A LOOK AT LIFE CYCLES

Insect Life Cycles

BY BRAY JACOBSON

Gareth Stevens PUBLISHING

CRASHCOURSE

Please visit our website, www.garethstevens.com. For a free color catalog of all our high-quality books, call toll free 1-800-542-2595 or fax 1-877-542-2596.

Cataloging-in-Publication Data
Names: Jacobson, Bray.
Title: Insect life cycles / Bray Jacobson.
Description: New York : Gareth Stevens Publishing, 2018. | Series: A look at life cycles | Includes index.
Identifiers: ISBN 9781538210444 (pbk.) | ISBN 9781538210468 (library bound) | ISBN 9781538210451 (6 pack)
Subjects: LCSH: Insects--Life cycles--Juvenile literature.
Classification: LCC QL467.2 J25 2018 | DDC 595.7156--dc23

First Edition

Published in 2018 by
Gareth Stevens Publishing
111 East 14th Street, Suite 349
New York, NY 10003

Designer: Samantha DeMartin
Editor: Kristen Nelson

Photo credits: Series art Im stocker/Shutterstock.com; cover, p. 1 beer worawut/Shutterstock.com; p. 5 Kimree/Shutterstock.com; p. 7 (ladybug) fragariavesca/Shutterstock.com; p. 7 (praying mantis) sparc/Shutterstock.com; p. 7 (rhinocerous beetle) JuRin GrooveRider/Shutterstock.com; p. 7 (dragonfly) Costea Andrea M/Shutterstock.com; p. 9 (leaf beetle eggs) undefined/Shutterstock.com; p. 9 (mosquito eggs) thatmacroguy/Shutterstock.com; p. 9 (ant eggs) boyphare/Shutterstock.com; p. 11 Lorenzo Sala/Shutterstock.com; p. 13 (main) Tsekhmister/Shutterstock.com; p. 13 (adult) Lena Aref/Shutterstock.com; p. 13 (nymph) Vitalii Hulai/Shutterstock.com; p. 13 (eggs) Patrick Rolands/Shutterstock.com; p. 15 MR. TEERSAK KHEMNGERN/Shutterstock.com; p. 17 Cathy Keifer/Shutterstock.com; pp. 19, 25 HHelene/Shutterstock.com; p. 21 D. Kucharski K. Kucharska/Shutterstock.com; p. 23 Saint Fuangnakhon/Shutterstock.com; p. 27 PorKaliver/Shutterstock.com; p. 29 ldrus/Shutterstock.com; p. 30 suns07butterfly/Shutterstock.com.

Printed in the United States of America

CPSIA compliance information: Batch #CW18GS: For further information contact Gareth Stevens, New York, New York at 1-800-542-2595.

Contents

Words in the glossary appear in **bold** type the first time they are used in the text.

Insects All Over

In order for an animal to be called an insect, it has to have three pairs of legs and antennae. Insects' bodies have three segments, or parts: head, **thorax**, and **abdomen**. They may or may not have one or two pairs of wings.

Make the Grade

Insects also have a hard outer covering on their body called an exoskeleton.

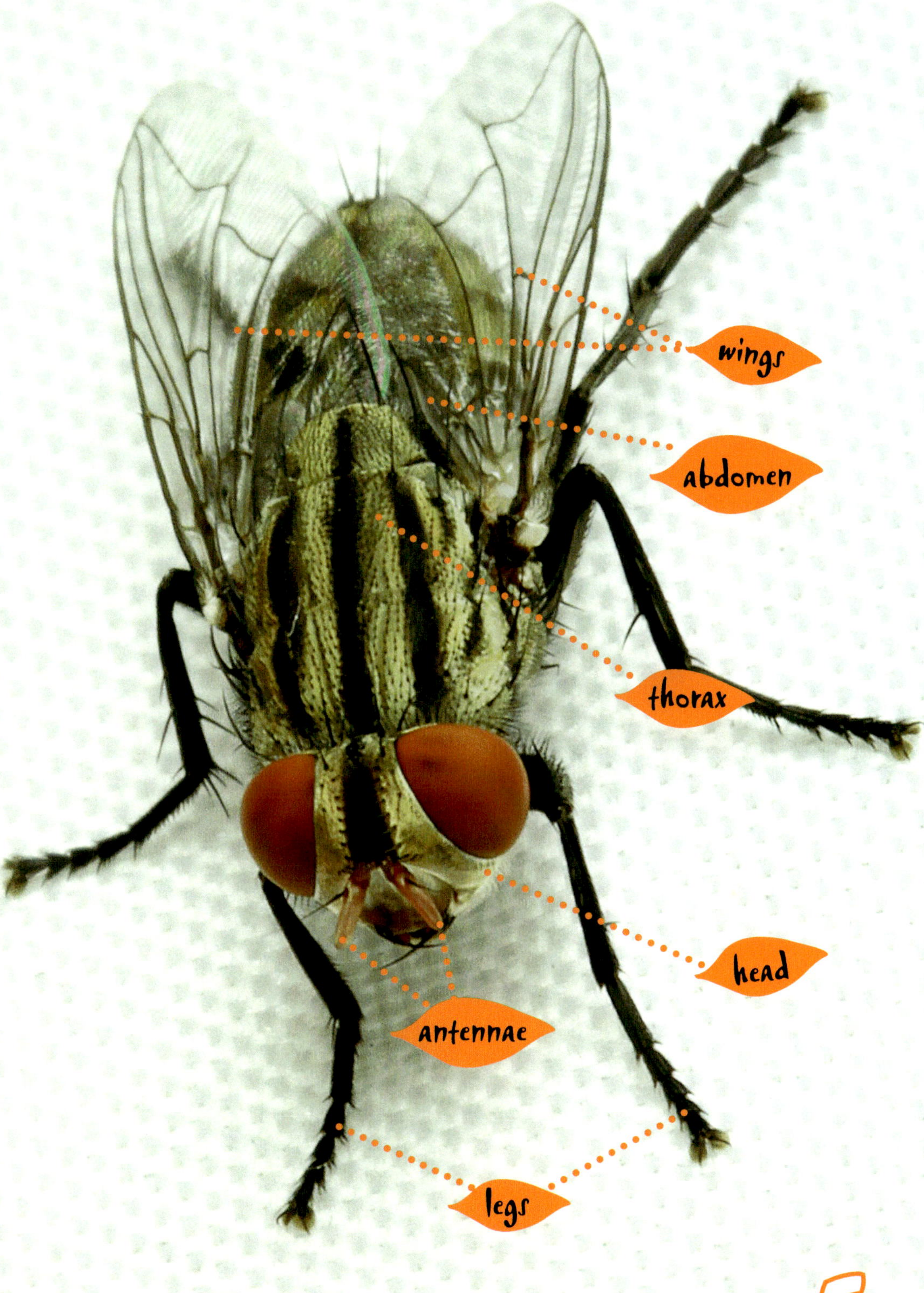
wings
abdomen
thorax
head
antennae
legs

There are so many kinds of insects on Earth, scientists aren't sure of the number! However, all insects have similar parts to their life cycle. A life cycle is the **stages** an animal goes through during its life.

Make the Grade

Insects have **adapted** their life cycle to help them **survive** where they live. For example, the length of each stage is different for each kind of insect!

ladybug

praying
mantis

rhinoceros
beetle

dragonfly

Get Hatching!

No matter the kind, all insects **hatch** from eggs. Many insect **species** lay eggs, whether on water, plants, or the ground. But some insects' eggs are kept inside the female's body until they hatch!

Make the Grade

Insect eggs may be too small to see or as long as 1/2 inch (1.3 cm)! Many eggs are white or gray, but they can also be brightly colored!

ant eggs

mosquito eggs

leaf beetle eggs

Second Stage

When most insects hatch, they're called larvae. Larvae look very different from one insect to the next! Some beetle larvae have legs, but no wings. Many flies' larvae have no legs and look like tiny worms!

Make the Grade

Some kinds of insects hatch from their eggs looking like tiny copies of adults!

When some insects reach their second life stage, they're called nymphs. Nymphs often look a lot like adults and may live in the same **habitat**. Many types of flying bugs that lay eggs in water have babies that are called naiads (NY-ads) after they hatch.

Make the Grade

Nymphs commonly eat the same things as adults of their species. Naiads and larvae don't because they don't often share a habitat with adults.

Life Cycle of a Dragonfly

Metamorphosis

How long an insect spends as a larva depends on its species. Some larvae form a case or cocoon around themselves. Now, these young insects are called pupae. Inside the case, the insect's body is changing into an adult.

Make the Grade

When an insect comes out of its pupal case, it will look very different from when it was a larva. This is called complete metamorphosis (meh-tuh-MOHR-fuh-suhs)!

Many insects don't have a pupal stage, but their bodies do still change before they're adults. They **shed** their exoskeleton, sometimes several times. This is called molting. With each molt, the insect grows bigger and may go through body changes, such as growing wings.

Make the Grade

Molting is another kind of metamorphosis because an insect's body is changing.

Roach Life

In order for the American cockroach's life cycle to start, a male and female cockroach must mate. About 3 to 7 days later, a female cockroach makes an egg case. She carries it for a few hours or days before hiding it to keep it safe!

Make the Grade

An insect, like other animals, must find another of its kind to mate, or produce babies, with.

Cockroach nymphs come out of their eggs after between 24 and 38 days. Now, they begin to grow and change by molting! Cockroach nymphs molt 10 to 13 times, growing wings and becoming able to **reproduce**.

Make the Grade

It takes 6 months to a year for a nymph to become an adult cockroach.

American cockroaches live about 1 year. A female cockroach will make as many as 14 egg cases during her life—and there may be as many as 15 baby cockroaches in each! Their life cycle moves quickly!

Make the Grade

When the conditions are right, cockroach populations can grow fast!

The Life Cycle of a Cockroach

Building a Butterfly

A female butterfly lays her eggs on the leaves or stems of plants. Over time, a larva grows inside each egg. It's called a caterpillar! The caterpillar eats its way out of the egg after a few weeks or when it's warm enough.

Make the Grade

Caterpillars eat a lot! Because of this, they outgrow their skin and molt four or five times after they come out of the egg.

Caterpillars may grow to be 100 times the size they were when they hatched! Once grown enough, they form themselves into a pupa. A hard case grows around them, too. It keeps them safe from predators and bad weather.

Make the Grade

The pupal stage of butterflies is often called the chrysalis.

A butterfly may stay a pupa for weeks or months, depending on what kind it is! Once the butterfly does come out, it doesn't fly right away. It needs to let its soft, wet wings dry out and become harder. It's now an adult!

Make the Grade

Some kinds of female butterflies get to choose which male to mate with. Sometimes, male butterflies mate with females before they're out of their chrysalis!

The Life Cycle of a Butterfly

Adult butterflies mate.

A female butterfly lays eggs.

Caterpillars hatch from the eggs.

The caterpillars eat a lot and grow.

Each caterpillar becomes a pupa.

Inside the pupa, the caterpillar changes over weeks or months.

A butterfly comes out of the pupal case!

Glossary

abdomen: the part of an insect's body that contains the stomach

adapt: to change to suit conditions

habitat: the place where an animal lives

hatch: to come out of

reproduce: when an animal creates another creature just like itself

shed: to lose an outer covering

species: a group of plants or animals that are all the same kind

stage: a step in the growth of an animal

survive: to live through something

thorax: the middle part of an insect's body. The wings and legs connect to it.

For More Information

Books

Amstutz, L. J. *Investigating Animal Life Cycles*. Minneapolis, MN: Lerner Publications, 2016.

Stewart, Melissa. *Zoom in on Butterflies*. Berkeley Heights, NJ: Enslow Publishers, 2014.

Websites

The Butterfly Life Cycle!

www.ngkids.co.uk/science-and-nature/butterfly-life-cycle

Find information, images, and illustrations to help review the butterfly's life cycle.

Publisher's note to educators and parents: Our editors have carefully reviewed these websites to ensure that they are suitable for students. Many websites change frequently, however, and we cannot guarantee that a site's future contents will continue to meet our high standards of quality and educational value. Be advised that students should be closely supervised whenever they access the Internet.

Index